A Homestay in Auckland

I Talk You Talk Press

CONTENTS

Introduction   1

1. An email to the host family   2

2. Arrival   4

3. The house   6

4. Dinner   9

5. The bathroom   12

6. The next morning   14

7. A new friend   17

8. Presents   19

9. Erina's first week   21

10. Sightseeing on Saturday   24

11. Sunday   27

12. Sunday evening and a traditional New Zealand dinner   29

13. Erina's second week   31

14. Saturday   34

15. Saying goodbye   36

Thank You   38

About the Author   39

INTRODUCTION

The words in **bold** are useful homestay phrases.

You might hear these phrases, and you can use some of these phrases when you go on a homestay.

Erina Adachi is a university student from Nagoya. She is nineteen years old. She studies English at university.

It is August. Erina is going on a homestay next week. She is going to New Zealand. She is going to stay with a host family in Auckland for two weeks. She is going to study at a language school in the city. Then, she is going to travel for four days. She is going to Queenstown.

1. AN EMAIL TO THE HOST FAMILY

Erina is excited. This morning, the homestay company sent her information about her host family. She reads the information. There is an email address.

I will send an email, thinks Erina. *It is good manners to send a mail or a letter to the host family before the homestay.*

She goes to her desk, and switches on her computer. She opens a new email, types in the host family's email address, and writes an email.

---Dear Mr and Mrs Williams, and Joanne,

My name is Erina Adachi. I will be staying with you for two weeks. I will arrive next Sunday.

It's my first time to leave Japan, and I'm very excited, but a little nervous.

I'd like to tell you a little about myself. I am 19 years old, and I live in Nagoya. I am a university student. I study English at university. There are 4 people in my family - my father, mother, younger brother and me. In my free time, I enjoy running. Last year, I ran my first marathon. I also like reading and listening to music.

How is the weather in Auckland now? Do I need to bring warm clothes? In Nagoya, it is summer, so it is very hot. I'm looking forward to meeting you next week.

From Erina Adachi.---

The next day, Erina got this reply from the Williams family.

---Dear Erina,

Thank you very much for your email. We hope you will have a wonderful time in New Zealand.

It is cool in August in Auckland. The daytime temperature is about 15 degrees, so you will need to bring some warm clothes.

Our daughter, Joanne, is very interested in Japan. She is studying Japanese. She is looking forward to talking to you. She will ask you many questions about Japan and Japanese culture!

We will meet you at the airport on Sunday. We will wait for you near the exit. We are looking forward to meeting you! Have a pleasant flight to NZ.

From Kath, Ted and Joanne Williams---

Erina reads the email again. *Joanne likes Japanese culture,* she thinks. *I hope I can answer all of her questions in English!*

2. ARRIVAL

The flight to Auckland from Narita is long. It takes about eleven hours.

Erina is sitting next to the window. The aeroplane is landing. She is very excited.

The flight attendant makes an announcement. She says, "Welcome to Auckland. The local time is 8:15 am."

Erina looks at her watch. It says 5:15 am. She is surprised. Then she remembers. *There is a time difference between New Zealand and Japan. I must change my watch!*

Erina gets off the plane and goes through immigration. Then she picks up her suitcase and waits in the line for customs and agriculture. Finally everything is finished, and she goes out into the arrivals hall.

Where are Mr and Mrs Williams? she thinks. She looks around. There are so many people!

Then she sees a man and a woman. The man is holding a large piece of paper. On the paper it says, "Erina Adachi".

Erina walks over to them.

"**Excuse me, are you** Mr and Mrs Williams?" she asks.

"Yes. Are you Erina?" asks Mrs Williams.

"Yes!"

"Welcome to New Zealand!" says Mrs Williams. They shake hands. "**Please call me** Kath."

"And please call me Ted," says Mr Williams.

"Thank you," says Erina.

Ted takes Erina's suitcase. They walk out of the airport.

"**How was your flight?**" asks Kath.

"**It was fine, thank you,**" says Erina.

"**Are you tired?**" asks Kath.

"**A little,**" says Erina. "I slept on the plane."

3. THE HOUSE

They get into the car. Ted drives the car along a wide road. Erina looks out of the window. She sees some sheep.

"Do you have sheep in Japan?" asks Kath.

"Yes, we do, but not so many," says Erina.

After about 25 minutes, they arrive at the Williams' house. It is very big with a large garden.

Ted parks the car in the driveway. He takes Erina's suitcase out of the car.

"Joanne is very excited. She is waiting to meet you," says Kath.

Ted carries Erina's suitcase into the house.

"**Should I take my shoes off?**" asks Erina.

We don't usually wear shoes in the house, but please yourself."

"In Japan we take our shoes off, so I will do the same here!" says Erina.

Joanne is waiting.

"Hi, Erina, I'm Joanne. *Konnichiwa!*" says Joanne.

"**Nice to meet you,**" says Erina. "And you speak Japanese!"

"Yes. A little. I want to speak Japanese with you," says Joanne.

"Let's practise later!" says Erina laughing. "How old are you?"

"I'm sixteen," says Joanne. "How old are you?"

"I'm nineteen," says Erina.

They walk into the living room.

Erina looks around the room. It is very large. There is a large sofa and two armchairs. There is a coffee table in the centre of the room and there is a large TV in the corner.

"**You have a very nice house.** It is very different from houses in Japan."

"Oh really?" says Kath. "**What is your house like?**"

"My family lives in an apartment. It is on the tenth floor, so we have a nice view of Nagoya. I have some photographs. Would you like to see them? I'll show them to you later."

"Thank you. We would love to see your photographs," says Ted.

"Erina, **would you like something to drink?**" asks Kath.

"**Yes, please. That would be very nice.**"

"We have coffee, tea, orange juice, mineral water, or herb tea. **What would you like?**"

"**Could I have a cup of tea, please? But first, could I use the bathroom?**"

"**Yes, of course.** We have a small bathroom downstairs. **I'll show you.**"

Kath shows Erina the bathroom.

When Erina comes back to the living room, Kath asks, "**Are you hungry?**"

"**A little,**" says Erina.

"It's lunchtime, so I'll make some sandwiches. Are ham sandwiches OK?"

"Yes, thank you," says Erina.

"I'll help you," says Joanne.

Kath and Joanne go out of the room.

"Please sit down," says Ted. "**Make yourself at home.** This is your home now, so please relax!"

"Thank you. I'm sorry, I'm a little nervous," says Erina.

"That's OK. Everyone is nervous at first when they stay in a new place."

Kath brings the drinks and sandwiches. She pours tea for everyone.

"Erina, **do you have milk and sugar in your tea?**"

"**Just milk, please.**"

Kath hands a cup of tea to Erina.

"Thank you," says Erina.

They drink the tea and eat the sandwiches.

"**How far are we from the centre of the city?**" asks Erina.

"Not so far," says Ted. "It's only a twenty minute drive."

"**Is there a bus from here to the city centre?**"

"Yes, there is. But I will take you to your school tomorrow. My office is very near your school," says Ted.

They talk about Japan and New Zealand. Then, Kath looks at Erina.

"Erina, you look tired. **Would you like to take a nap before dinner?**" asks Kath.

"A nap? **I'm sorry, I don't understand that word. What does** nap **mean?**" asks Erina.

"A nap is a short sleep, or rest," says Ted.

"Oh I see. **Yes, I'd like that. What time should I wake up?**"

"**We'll eat dinner at** about six thirty."

"OK. I'll set my alarm clock," says Erina.

"Come with me, I'll show you your room. It's upstairs. Please bring your shoes," says Kath.

"My shoes?" asks Erina.

"Yes, we take our shoes to our rooms," says Kath. "We leave gardening shoes and work boots outside the back door, but we always put other shoes in our bedrooms."

"Oh, I see. In Japan, we leave our shoes at the door," says Erina.

Kath and Erina walk up the stairs.

Kath points to a door. "This is Joanne's bedroom." She points to another door. "This is a bathroom. You and Joanne will share this bathroom. Ted and I have another small bathroom next to our bedroom. And here is your room," says Kath.

They walk into the bedroom. It is very large. There is a big bed next to the window. There is a desk and a chair in the corner. Erina looks around.

"**It's very nice. Thank you.**" She goes to the window and looks out. She can see the garden.

Kath opens a closet door. "**You can hang your clothes in here.**" We hope you will be comfortable here."

"I'm sure I will be very comfortable," answers Erina.

Kath smiles. "Have a good rest," she says.

"Thank you," says Erina.

Kath walks out of the room and closes the door. Erina opens her suitcase. She takes out her alarm clock.

She changes the time to New Zealand time and sets the alarm to 6:00pm. Then she lies down on the bed. Very soon, she falls asleep.

4. DINNER

The alarm clock is ringing. Erina wakes up. It is 6:00pm. She goes downstairs. Everyone is in the living room watching TV.

"**Did you sleep well?**" asks Ted.

"**Yes, thank you. I slept very well,**" says Erina.

"I'm sure you were very tired," says Ted.

"Yes, I was!" says Erina.

"Are you hungry?" asks Kath.

"Yes, I am a little," says Erina. She is very hungry.

"Do you like pizza? I made a pizza while you were sleeping."

"Yes, I love pizza. Thank you," says Erina.

"It will be ready in about ten minutes," says Kath.

"Er, **could I ask a favour?**" asks Erina.

"**Sure. What is it?**" asks Kath.

"**Would it be OK if I sent an email** to my mother and father? I think they will be worried about me."

"Oh yes of course! The computer is in Ted's office. You can send an email anytime. But tonight, maybe your parents want to hear your voice. Why don't you call them?"

"But that is very expensive for you. An email will be fine," says Erina.

"It's OK. We don't want your parents to worry about you. Here is the phone. Do you know how to make international calls to Japan?" asks Kath.

"No, I don't."

"OK, I'll show you. First you press zero twice. Then eight one for

Japan and then the area code for Nagoya. What is the area code for Nagoya?"

"It's zero five two," says Erina.

"Well, you don't need the zero. So please press zero zero eight one five two and then your family's telephone number."

"OK, thank you." Erina dials the number and talks to her family. When she has finished, Kath says, "How are your mother and father?"

"They are fine, thank you. They are happy I arrived safely. **Thank you for letting me make the phone call.** I know it is expensive, so I won't call again. I will email them," says Erina.

"You can email them anytime. But if you want to talk to your parents, you can call them again. Or maybe you can use the computer. Do your parents have Skype?"

"They don't use Skype, but my younger brother does. They could use his computer."

"Is the pizza ready?" asks Ted. "I'm hungry!"

They all go into the dining room. There is a large table in the middle of the room.

"**Where should I sit?**" asks Erina.

"**You can sit here,**" says Ted. "This seat has a view of the garden."

Erina sits down. Joanne sits down opposite her. Ted brings some glasses, plates and a bottle of water. Kath brings a salad and pizza.

"Let's eat!" says Ted.

"**Help yourself to** salad," says Kath.

"**Thank you,**" says Erina.

She takes some salad and passes the bowl to Joanne. Then, she takes a slice of pizza and eats it.

"This is delicious!" she says.

"Thank you," says Kath.

"Kath is a good cook," says Ted.

Joanne asks Erina many questions about Japan. Joanne has been studying Japanese for three years. Erina is surprised.

"Where do you study Japanese?" she asks.

"At school," says Joanne.

"Is your teacher Japanese?" asks Erina.

"No. Some schools have teachers from Japan, but our teacher is a New Zealander. She lived in Japan for a long time. She lived in

Tokyo."

"Oh, I see," says Erina.

They all finish eating.

"Would you like some dessert?" asks Kath.

"Yes, please," says Erina.

"I made some chocolate cake," says Kath.

"Oh wonderful!" says Erina. "I love chocolate cake."

"Good! I hope you like this!"

"I'm sure I will," says Erina.

Erina takes a bite of the cake.

"This is very nice!" she says.

"Thank you," says Kath. "Erina, we need to talk about food. We will make breakfast and dinner for you every day. You can make sandwiches for lunch, or you can buy something in the city centre. We always have sandwich bread, and there is ham and cheese in the refrigerator. Help yourself to fruit too. **Is there any food you don't like?"**

"I like everything," says Erina.

"Do you have any allergies?"

"No, I don't."

"Is there any New Zealand food you would like to eat?"

"I don't know much about New Zealand food, but **I would like to try** everything."

"OK, we will make you some traditional New Zealand dishes."

"Thank you very much," says Erina.

"What do you usually have for breakfast?" asks Ted.

"I usually have egg, toast and yoghurt," says Erina. "But I will have the same as you."

"We usually eat cereal, fruit, yoghurt and toast. But I can cook eggs for you. It's no trouble," says Kath.

"Cereal, fruit, yoghurt and toast will be fine for me, thank you," says Erina.

5. THE BATHROOM

After dinner, everyone is in the living room. Erina is feeling very tired, and she wants to take a bath.

"Kath, **do you have a bath in this house?**" she asks.

"Yes, of course. The bathroom upstairs has a bath."

"**Is it OK if I take a bath?**"

"Oh yes, of course. Do you always take a bath in the evening?" asks Kath.

"Yes, I do. How about you?"

"We all take a shower in the morning. Or if I have a busy day at work, I take a bath in the evening to relax. Sometimes Joanne takes a bath too."

"**Is it OK if I take a bath every evening after dinner?**"

"Yes, of course. You can use the bathroom any time it is free. I'll show you how to use the bath and shower now."

They walk up the stairs and go into the bathroom. It is very large. There is a toilet, sink, shower and a bath.

"This is the shower. You can change the temperature by turning this handle. And this is the bath. Just turn the taps on."

"**Where should I put my wet towel?**" asks Erina.

"You can put it on this stand here."

"**Is it OK if I leave my wash bag in the bathroom?**"

"Yes, of course." Kath points to a shelf next to the window. "This is your shelf. You can leave it here."

"Thank you," says Erina.

Erina has a bath and gets ready for bed. She goes down to the living room to say goodnight to everyone.

"**I think I'll go to bed now,**" says Erina. "**I'm feeling very tired.**"

"**What time does school start tomorrow morning?**" asks Kath.

"**It starts at** nine am," says Erina. "**What time do you usually get up?**"

"**We usually get up at** seven am," says Ted.

"OK, **I'll get up around** seven am tomorrow," says Erina. "**Good night.**"

"Good night!" says everyone. "**Sleep well!**"

Erina goes up to her room and gets into bed. The she remembers.

I have presents for Ted, Kath and Joanne! I forgot to give them the presents! What should I do? I will give them the presents tomorrow evening. It's too late now.

She falls asleep very quickly.

6. THE NEXT MORNING

The next morning, Erina wakes up at 6:45. She slept very well, so she feels very refreshed. She gets up and goes to the bathroom. Then she gets dressed.

She goes downstairs. Everyone is still sleeping.

Should I start making breakfast? she thinks.

Kath comes downstairs.

"**Good morning! Did you sleep well?**" she asks.

"**Yes, I slept very well, thank you. Did you?**"

"Yes, I did," says Kath. "I'm sorry, I forgot to show you the coffee and bread. The coffee is in this cupboard, and the bread is here. The eggs, milk and yoghurt are in the fridge. The fruit is here, in this basket. **Help yourself.**"

"Thank you. **Where are the cups?**" asks Erina.

"**They are here,**" says Kath.

"**Shall I** make the coffee?" asks Erina.

"Oh, yes please. Thank you. I'll set the table, and make toast."

There is a table in the kitchen. Kath puts cereal boxes, fruit juice, butter and honey on the table. There is a small TV on the wall. Kath switches it on.

"I like to check the weather forecast," she says.

Ted and Joanne get up. Everyone sits around the kitchen table and eats breakfast. They watch the morning news on TV.

After breakfast, Erina says, "**I'll help you with the washing up.**"

"No it's OK. I will do it. I'm not working today," says Kath. "Do you want to make some sandwiches to take to school?"

"I don't know," says Erina. "Are there any restaurants near the school?"

"There are many small restaurants and lunch bars near the school. You can even buy sushi!" says Ted. "But eating out is expensive. So please think about taking lunch from here."

"OK. Thank you. But today is my first day, so I'll buy lunch. **I'd like to practise my English**," says Erina.

"I'll take you to school," says Ted.

"**That is a lot of trouble for you**," says Erina.

"It's no trouble. My office is near your school," says Ted.

"**What time will we leave?**" asks Erina.

"We'll leave at eight o clock and get to the school at around eight twenty-five. I start work at nine so we have to go early."

"That's fine. **I'll be ready by** eight," says Erina.

Erina looks out of the window. It is very sunny.

"**Will it be cool today?**"

"Yes, it will be quite cool. It's sunny but a little windy. You will need a jacket," says Ted.

Erina and Ted leave at 8:00.

"**See you later!**" says Kath. "**Have a good day!**"

"You too! **See you later!**" says Erina.

"**What time do you finish school?**" asks Ted.

"**I finish at** five," says Erina.

"**I'll pick you up** outside the school entrance at five ten. I finish work at five. It will take me ten minutes to get to the school."

"That's great, thank you very much," says Erina. "What do you do?"

"I work in a bank," says Ted.

"Oh really? My father works in an office."

"Oh I see," says Ted. "Does your mother work?"

"Yes, she's a teacher," says Erina. "What does Kath do?"

"She's a writer."

"A writer? That's interesting. What does she write? Does she write books?"

"No, not books. She writes magazine articles about food and cooking. She is also a chef."

"I see! Her cooking is very nice. The pizza last night was good."

"Yes, she is a good cook. I think you will eat a lot of food while you are here. You will need to go on a diet when you go back to

Japan!" says Ted.

Erina laughs. "That's OK. I want to eat lots of New Zealand food while I'm here."

Ted stops the car outside a large building on a busy street. There are many people wearing suits. They are going to work. There are many cars and buses on the road too.

"This is the language school," he says. "I'll pick you up here at five ten. If I'm not here, just wait."

"OK, thank you," says Erina. She gets out of the car.

"Good luck! Enjoy your day!" says Ted.

Erina waves. **"You too!"** Then, she walks into the school.

7. A NEW FRIEND

Erina has a good first day. There are seven other students in her class. She is the only Japanese student, so she has to speak English with the other students. Three of the students are from China, two are from Korea, one is from Somalia and another is from Russia.

Everyone is very friendly. They study in the morning, and then they have lunch. The school has a small lunch room. The students can make tea or coffee there. Erina goes out of the language school. There is a sandwich shop next door. She buys a packet of sandwiches and goes back to the school. In the afternoon, the students have more classes.

At 5:00, Erina walks out of the school and waits outside with Soo-jin, her new friend from Korea. Soo-jin's host father will also pick her up outside the school.

"What is your host family like?" asks Soo-jin.

"They are very kind. Their house is very big," says Erina. "How about yours?"

"They are very nice too. They have two young children. They are very cute."

"My host family has a daughter. She is sixteen. She studies Japanese! I was very surprised!" says Erina.

"Really? That's interesting!" says Soo-jin.

"Yes, and…" Erina stops. She sees Ted's car.

"Oh, I'm sorry. Here is my host father!" says Erina. "I have to go! See you tomorrow!"

"See you tomorrow!" says Soo-jin.

Erina gets in the car.

"**How was your day?**" asks Ted.

"**It was good! I made some new friends and I studied a lot! How about you? How was your day?**"

"Oh, **my day was fine.** The same as usual!"

There are many cars on the road. It is the rush hour, so it takes around forty minutes to get home.

8. PRESENTS

They arrive home. Kath and Joanne are waiting.

"We're back!" says Ted.

They walk into the living room.

"**Hi! Welcome back! How was your day** Erina? **Did you have a nice time?**" asks Kath.

"**Yes, I had a very good time. I made some new friends.**"

"Are there any other Japanese students in your class?" asks Kath.

"No, there aren't. That is good for me. I have to speak English. I can't speak any Japanese! Kath, **do you have free time now?**" asks Erina.

"Yes, we do," says Kath.

"**I have some presents for you** from Japan," says Erina.

"Oh thank you!"

Erina goes to her room and picks up the bag of presents. Then, she goes to the living room.

She takes out a box and gives it to Kath. "**This is for you,**" she says. "**I hope you will like it.**"

Kath opens it. "Oh, this is very nice! A fan! Thank you!"

"And this is for you," says Erina, giving a box to Ted.

"Thank you," he says.

He opens the box. "Oh, a Japanese baseball cap! This is wonderful. Thank you!" Ted puts the cap on.

"And this is for you Joanne," says Erina.

She gives Joanne a present. Joanne opens it. "Manga!" she says. "Thank you! I can practise reading Japanese!"

"And these are cookies for you all," says Erina.

She puts the cookies on the table. "I hope you like them. They are matcha green tea flavour."

"Oh, we love matcha, thank you," says Kath.

"Can we open them?" asks Joanne.

"Let's save them for a special occasion," says Kath. "Erina, **have you had** whitebait before?"

"Whitebait? I don't know. What is it?"

"A kind of fish. A neighbour went fishing. He caught a lot of whitebait and gave some to me. I'm going to cook them for dinner. **Would you like to try them?**"

"Yes, please."

"OK, **dinner will be ready in** about half an hour. **Relax and watch some TV while you wait.**"

"Is it OK if I use the computer? **I'd like to** check my email."

"Yes, of course. You don't need to ask," says Ted.

"Thank you," says Erina.

Erina checks her email and then everyone goes into the dining room. They sit down. The whitebait are very small fish. Kath mixed them with egg and flour and fried them. They have French fries, salad and fruit too. Everything tastes good.

"Thank you very much," says Erina. **"The meal was delicious."**

Kath smiles. **"I'm glad you liked it."**

"Can I help you clear the table, or help with the dishes?" asks Erina.

"Oh, thank you. That's very kind of you. Yes, you can dry the dishes."

Joanne starts to take the plates and dishes into the kitchen. Erina helps her. Joanne washes the dishes and Erina dries them.

"Do you always wash the dishes?" asks Erina.

"Yes, that's my job," says Joanne. "Do Japanese children wash dishes too?"

"I think some children do," says Erina. "But my mother always washes the dishes in my house."

9. ERINA'S FIRST WEEK

Erina is very happy. Ted takes her to school every day. He picks her up after school. Every night Kath cooks delicious food for dinner. In the evenings, Erina studies for her classes the next day. Joanne comes into her room every evening to talk. They speak in English and Japanese.

Erina is learning a lot. She speaks English all day. She speaks English with Ted and Kath and Joanne. She is learning some other things too.

One night, Kath says "We're having pumpkin soup and quiche and salad tonight. I hope you like it."

"I like all your cooking," says Erina.

Kath serves the soup. She doesn't put any more food on the table. Erina thinks it is strange. Erina waits. She looks around. Everyone else has finished their soup. They are waiting for her to finish.

"Oh, I'm sorry. In Japan all the dishes are put on the table together. I was waiting for the rest of the meal!"

Everyone laughs. "That's OK," says Ted. "I guess we do some things differently. Usually we have the soup first. Then when everyone is finished, the next part of the meal comes."

Joanne talks to Erina about her school life. She shows Erina her school books. Erina thinks it is very interesting. Joanne is studying hard because she will have tests soon, but she seems to have more free time than Japanese students. Joanne plays soccer and she takes jazz ballet classes.

The students in Erina's class eat lunch together every day.

On Thursday, Soo-jin says, "How about we take our lunch to the park today? We can ask Min-ji to come too."

Min-ji is the other Korean student in their class.

"OK," says Erina. "That would be nice."

There is a small park near the school. The three girls take their lunches and walk to the park. It is a little cold, and Erina is pleased she has her warm jacket. They sit on a park bench. Very soon, some birds come close to them.

"They want our lunch!" says Soo-jin.

Then she says to Min-ji, "Min-ji, I don't think you are very happy. What's wrong?"

"It's my host family," says Min-ji. "They are very nice people. They are very kind. But they don't talk to me."

Erina is surprised. "What do you mean? They don't talk to you?"

Soo-jin is surprised too. "They don't say anything to you?"

"They talk to me a little," says Min-ji. "They ask me about my day. They ask 'Did you have a good day?' 'Is the food OK?' 'Are you happy?' But I never have a conversation. They have two teenage children. A boy and a girl. I want to talk to them but they don't talk to me."

"Er, Min-ji," says Erina. "Do you talk to them?"

"Of course. When they ask me a question, I always say 'yes' or 'no' or 'thank you'."

"But Min-ji, do you ask them about their day? Do you ask the children about their school?"

"No. My English is not very good. And I'm shy."

"You have to answer a question, and then add something more," says Soo-jin. "If you only say yes or no, there is no conversation."

"But what should I say?" Min-ji is unhappy.

Erina takes her notebook and pen out of her bag. "We'll make you a list and we will practise with you!"

"Imagine! I am your homestay mother," says Soo-jin. "Hi, Min-ji. Did you have a good day?"

"Yes, thank you," says Min-ji.

"No, no!" says Erina. "Yes, thank you. I had lunch in the park with my friends. How was your day?"

"Now I am your homestay brother," says Soo-jin. "Speak to me, Erina!"

"Hi, Peter. How was school today?"

"It was OK. I had soccer practise."

"Will you play a game soon? I would like to come and watch!"

Soo-jin and Erina are laughing but then Soo-jin is serious again. "Min-ji, I understand it is hard, but you must try to make conversation. You can ask your homestay brother and sister about music. You can ask them if you can listen to their favourite music. You can ask your homestay mother if you can go to the supermarket with her. People will give up if you only say 'yes' or 'no'."

"OK, thank you for your advice. I will try," says Min-ji.

Erina looks at her watch. "Quick. We're going to be late for class. We have to hurry!"

10. SIGHTSEEING ON SATURDAY

On Friday afternoon, the students visit the Auckland museum. It is in a very large park full of trees, gardens and sports fields. They learn about New Zealand culture and history. A group performs some traditional music and dances. It is very interesting and Erina has a nice time. She goes back to the language school, and at 5:10, Ted picks her up and takes her back home.

"**What did you do today?**" asks Kath.

"**We went to** the museum."

"Oh, **how was it?**"

"**It was wonderful.** We watched some traditional singing and dancing."

"Yes, it's a very interesting place," says Kath. "**What are your plans for the weekend,** Erina?"

"**We are going** sightseeing with our teacher tomorrow. We are going to take a bus tour along the coast. **I have to be at the school at** 8:30am. It is early, and it is Saturday, so I can get the bus."

"I can drive you, Erina," says Ted.

"Thank you. That is very kind of you, but it is your day off, and **I'd like to try getting the bus. It will be a good experience for me.**"

"OK, that's fine."

"**Is there a bus stop near your house?**"

"Yes, there is one near the end of this street. There is a bus into the city every thirty minutes. The bus number is five hundred. I think you should catch the seven thirty bus. The bus will stop close to the Transport Centre. It is only about five minutes' walk from there to your school. You will get to the school in time," says Ted.

"**Take our phone number and address just in case you have any problems,**" says Kath.

"**Thank you,**" says Erina. "**I'm sure I'll be fine.**"

"**What time will you come back?**"

"The tour is four hours," says Erina. "So I will be back in the city centre by about one o'clock."

"**Do you want me to pick you up?**" asks Ted.

"**That's very kind of you, but I would like to get the bus back too,**" says Erina.

"OK. But if you have any problems you must call us. We will help you."

The next morning, Erina waits at the bus stop. She gets on the bus and says to the driver, "**To Britomart Transport Centre, please. How much is it?**"

"It's four dollars fifty," says the driver. Erina pays, and sits down and looks out of the window. She gets off the bus at the Transport Centre and walks to the school.

Erina has a nice day sightseeing with her class. They go to Manukau Harbour and to a rain forest. They walk along a beach. The scenery is beautiful. She takes many photographs and buys some souvenirs for her family and friends. The tour bus takes them back to the transport centre.

Erina looks around. She sees the number 500 bus.

"**Does this bus go to Ellerslie?**" she asks the driver.

"**Yes, it does.**"

She pays and sits down.

She looks out of the window until she sees her stop. She gets off the bus and walks from the main street down a smaller street.

All the streets look the same. She looks at the street sign. It says Pipitea Street.

Oh no! This isn't Patea Street. This is Pipitea! Where is Patea Street? she thinks.

She cannot see Patea Street. She sees a woman with a child in a garden. She takes out the host family's address. She shows it to the woman.

25

"**Excuse me, could you tell me how to get to** Patea Street **please?**"

The woman looks at the address. "Yes, it's very near. Go to the end of the street and turn right. Then, take the second left."

"Thank you very much," says Erina.

"**You're welcome,**" says the woman.

Erina arrives home.

"How was your day?" asks Kath.

"It was very nice. But, when I got off the bus, I walked the wrong way. I got lost!"

"Oh no! Why didn't you call us?"

"It was OK. I saw a woman in a garden, and she helped me. It was a good experience! I used my English!" says Erina.

"That was lucky! But if you have any trouble, you should call us!" says Kath.

Later, after dinner, everyone is sitting in the living room.

"**What do you usually do on Sundays?**" asks Erina.

"**I usually** work in the garden," says Ted.

"I usually go to the supermarket and then in the afternoon, I relax," says Kath. "**Would you like me to take you somewhere?**"

"**Please don't do anything special for me. But I would like to** see a supermarket. **May I come with you?**"

Kath laughs. "Of course! I don't think it will be very interesting, but you are very welcome to come with me. **Then what would you like to do in the afternoon?**"

"Erina could come out with me," says Joanne. "I am meeting my friends and we are going shopping."

"**I would like that very much, thank you,**" says Erina.

"I can introduce you to my friends," says Joanne. "We usually go to clothes shops."

"I'd like to see New Zealand fashion," says Erina. "**I'm looking forward to it!**"

11. SUNDAY

The next day, Erina gets up at 8:00am. Kath is in the kitchen. Ted and Joanne are still asleep.

Erina gets some coffee and sits down next to Kath.

"Kath, **I need to wash some clothes. Could I use the washing machine please?**"

"**Of course. Do you have a lot to wash?**"

"**Just a few things.**"

Kath stands up and says, "Come into the laundry and I'll show you." Erina and Kath go to a small room near the back of the house.

"This is the washing machine," says Kath. "And this is the drier. It is going to rain today, so you can't hang your clothes outside."

"**Could you show me how to use the washing machine please?**"

"Sure. This is the soap powder. Put it in here, then press this button and then press start."

"Thank you," says Erina. "I'll get my clothes."

When Erina's clothes are washed, and she has put them in the drier, Kath and Erina go to the supermarket.

Erina enjoys it very much. Erina knows most of the fruit and vegetables in the supermarket, but she is surprised to see so much cheese. There is a lot of international food too.

"Oh, look Kath!" says Erina. "They have Japanese food!"

"Yes. Japanese food is popular in New Zealand. Most supermarkets sell some Japanese food. You can buy noodles, miso, dried seaweed and some sauces."

In the afternoon, Erina goes shopping with Joanne and her friends. Her friends are very nice. Erina asks them many questions about their school life.

12. SUNDAY EVENING AND A TRADITIONAL NEW ZEALAND DINNER

Erina and Joanne come back from shopping. Kath is in the kitchen.

"We are going to eat a very traditional dinner tonight," she says.

"What are we having?" asks Joanne.

"Roast lamb," answers Kath.

"Oh, good!" Joanne is happy. "I love roast lamb!"

"**It will be ready at seven,**" says Kath.

"**Can I do anything to help you?**" asks Erina.

"No. But thank you. Why don't you relax? Ted worked hard in the garden all day. He got tired. He is asleep in front of the TV. I will wake him up soon."

Erina goes to check her emails. She reads an email from her mother and another from a friend. She has just finished answering the emails when Kath calls her.

"Erina! **Dinner is on the table!**"

Erina goes to the dining room. Ted is cutting a large piece of meat into slices. There are bowls of vegetables, a bowl of green sauce and a jug of gravy.

"**It smells wonderful,**" says Erina.

"**Help yourself,**" says Kath.

Erina takes meat, potato, pumpkin, sweet potato, peas and beans.

Joanne passes the jug of gravy to Erina. "Have some gravy," she says.

"And mint sauce!" says Ted. He passes the bowl.

"**Would you like some wine?**" asks Ted.

"Yes please," says Erina. "**But just a little.**"

Erina looks at the food on her plate. There is a lot.

I hope I can eat it all, she thinks.

The meal is delicious, but Erina can't eat everything on her plate.

"**I'm very sorry. I can't finish it. It all tastes so good, but maybe I took too much.**"

"That's OK," says Kath. "This meal is very different from Japanese food. Maybe it tastes a little strange."

"No, no. **I like it a lot. But I don't usually eat so much** meat."

"Don't worry," says Ted kindly. "We are glad you enjoyed it."

13. ERINA'S SECOND WEEK

On Monday morning Ted says to Erina, "I'm sorry. I'm going to work in another bank this week. It is about 50km south of here. So I can't take you to school, or drive you home. Can you take the bus?"

"Oh, yes," answers Erina.

"Please call if you are going to be late back from school," says Kath. "And promise me you will call if you have any problems."

"Yes, I will. I promise," says Erina. "But **I am sure I won't have any problems.**"

Erina is feeling very good. She has been in New Zealand for eight days. *My English is much better,* she thinks. *It was a good idea to come here.*

Erina takes the bus to school every day. The school is fun. Sometimes the classes are a little difficult, but Erina works hard. She studies every night. On Wednesday, school finishes a little early so Soo-jin, Min-ji and Erina go shopping. They go to the souvenir shop near the school. They buy souvenirs for their friends and families. Erina enjoys it a lot. But then she sees the clock in the shop.

"It's almost six o'clock!" she says. "I will be late!"

"Relax," says Min-ji. "Why don't you call? Just tell your host mother you will be back a little late."

"Yes," says Erina. "I will do that."

Erina calls Kath. "Hi, Kath," says Erina. "This is Erina. **I went shopping with my friends. The time passed so quickly** and I missed my usual bus. **I will be back around** seven pm. **Will that be OK?"**

"Of course!" answers Kath. "It's no problem. Thank you for calling."

On Thursday, the teacher says, "Tomorrow is your last day."

Oh no! thinks Erina. She likes her classmates and her teachers a lot. Time passes too quickly! I'm going to miss everyone so much.

After classes on Thursday, the students talk to each other. Everyone is sad. They enjoyed studying together.

"We will have our last class tomorrow," says Sergei, the Russian student. "After class, why don't we have a farewell party? We can go out to a restaurant."

Everyone thinks it is a good idea.

Erina is excited. When she gets back to her host family's house, she tells Kath.

"Tomorrow night, our class will go to a restaurant. We will have a farewell party! So **I will not be here for dinner.**"

"That will be nice for you," says Kath. "**Thank you for telling me.** There are not so many buses late at night. Please call when your party is finished. I will pick you up."

"That is a lot of trouble for you," says Erina. "I am sure I can take a bus."

"Yes, maybe you can. But **I will be very happy to come,**" says Kath.

"**In that case, thank you,**" says Erina.

On Friday night, the class goes to a restaurant near the school. It is very nice. It is self-service so everyone can choose their favourite food.

"Ooh. I ate too much!" says Soo-jin. "But I am going to eat some dessert. How about you Erina?"

"I ate a lot too. But I'd like to eat some fruit."

Erina finds the fresh fruit. Next to the fruit are big plates full of cheese. Erina looks at them.

A man standing next to Erina says, "Do you like cheese?"

"A little. But there are so many different kinds of cheese here. What is this cheese? It is a very strange colour."

The man laughs. "It's blue cheese. I like blue cheese very much. Why don't you try some?"

He takes a plate and puts a very small piece of the blue cheese on it. He gives the plate to Erina.

"Try it," he says.

Erina eats the piece of cheese.

"Do you like it?" asks the man.

Erina doesn't like it. "Hmm, **the taste is a little strong for me,**" she says.

The man laughs. "I understand," he says. "It has a very strong taste. Some people like it and some people don't like it."

Erina takes some fresh fruit and goes back to her friends. They are exchanging email addresses. Everyone is a little sad, but they have a great party.

14. SATURDAY

On Saturday morning, Erina has an idea. She goes to Joanne's room. She knocks on the door. "Joanne," she says. "It's Erina. **May I come in?**"

Joanne opens the door. She is studying.

"I have an idea," says Erina. "When I went to the supermarket with your mother, I saw some Japanese food. So, **I'd like to cook something tonight.**"

"That's a great idea," says Joanne. "Can I help?"

"**I hope you can help me. Are you busy today? Do you have time to** go to the supermarket with me?"

"Yes, of course. It will be fun.

Erina talks to Kath. "You cooked wonderful food for me. **Is it OK if I cook something for you tonight?**"

"Yes, of course. It will be very interesting," answers Kath. "Thank you. We always like to try new food."

Erina cooks fried noodles with pork and vegetables.

"What is this?" asks Joanne.

"It's yakisoba," says Erina. "Everyone has a different recipe, but this is how my mother makes it."

"It's very good," says Ted. "**May I have some more?**"

Erina is very happy. Ted and Kath and Joanne like her yakisoba.

"**I'm glad you like it,**" she says.

Erina," says Joanne. "Can we see the photographs of your family?"

Erina brings the photos. "**This is** my brother. He's in high school.

And **this is a picture of** my parents at my high school graduation ceremony."

"I want to know more about your hometown," says Joanne. "Can you show us your house on Google Earth?"

"Sure, I'll show you after dinner."

They go into the living room.

"Let's open the matcha cookies," says Joanne She opens them and passes them around.

"Oh, these are very nice, Erina, thank you," says Ted.

"I'm glad you like them," says Erina.

Ted brings an iPad from his office and Erina finds her apartment building on Google Earth.

"Here it is," she says.

"Oh, it's in the middle of the city! Do you like living there?" asks Kath.

"Yes, I do. It's very convenient. And I can go to Tokyo and Osaka and other cities very easily."

"Is it noisy?"

"Yes, it is, but I don't mind it," says Erina.

"So our house and neighbourhood are very quiet for you!" says Ted.

"Yes! It is very quiet here. But I like this too."

"I'd love to go to Japan," says Joanne.

"Please come! You can stay at my house!" says Erina.

"Really? Thank you! Can I go this year?" asks Joanne.

"Joanne! You are still at school! You can go when you finish school," says Ted.

"I want to climb Mount Fuji! Have you ever climbed Mount Fuji, Erina?" asks Joanne.

"No, I haven't, but if you come to Japan, we can climb it together!"

"Wow! I can't wait!" says Joanne.

When Erina goes to bed, she feels a little sad. Tomorrow will be her last night with the family. She wants to stay longer.

A two-week homestay is too short! she thinks. *Time passes too quickly!*

15. SAYING GOODBYE

It is Sunday night. Erina will leave Auckland tomorrow.

"**What time is your flight to** Queenstown tomorrow, Erina?" asks Ted.

"It's at 10:15. But I have to be at the airport at 9:15."

"I have to work tomorrow, but Kath can take you to the airport," says Ted.

"Thank you," says Erina.

The next morning, Erina says goodbye to Ted before he goes to work.

"**Thank you for letting me stay,**" she says. "**I had a wonderful time.**"

"**You're welcome.** We had a wonderful time too. Have a nice flight back to Japan. **I hope you come to stay with us again.**"

"**Thank you. I hope so too,**" says Erina.

Then, she says goodbye to Joanne. "I had a really nice time with you and your friends, Joanne. You can come and stay with me in Japan anytime. Just email me!"

"Thank you! I will! **Are you on Facebook?**"

"Yes I am. **I'll send you a friend request** when I get back to Japan!"

"Great! Let's be friends! My friends and I will visit you in Nagoya. Maybe next year?"

Erina laughs. "Any time is OK!"

Erina and Kath drive to the airport.

Erina takes her suitcase out of the car, and they walk into the departures lounge.

"**We will miss you,** Erina," says Kath.

"**I will miss you too,**" says Erina. "**I had a wonderful time here with you. Thank you for everything.**"

"**You're welcome.** If you have any problems in Queenstown, please call us. We will help you."

"Thank you," says Erina.

"**And please keep in touch. You have our email address.**"

"**I will. I promise. I'll write to you when I get back to** Japan. **And please come and visit me!** My family would like to meet you. You can stay in our apartment."

"Thank you, that's very kind of you."

"Goodbye," says Erina.

"Goodbye! **Have a safe trip** to Queenstown, and then a safe trip back to Japan! **Please say hello to** your parents **for me!**" says Kath.

"I will do! Thank you! Bye!"

An hour later, Erina gets on the aeroplane. She looks out of the window. The aeroplane takes off. She watches the houses become smaller and smaller.

She thinks about the past two weeks. She stayed with a nice family. She ate lots of New Zealand food. She got the bus, she went sightseeing, she studied English and she made some new friends.

It was a great experience, she thinks. *And now, I am going to Queenstown. I will stay in a hotel, and I will be alone for a few days. I hope I can speak lots of English and make some more friends.* Erina closes her eyes and falls asleep.

THANK YOU

Thank you for reading A Homestay in Auckland. (Word count: 8,087) We hope you enjoyed Erina Adachi's story. Other books in the Useful Phrases series are A Trip to London and A Business Trip to New York.

There is a quiz about the homestay phrases in this book on our free study site I Talk You Talk Press EXTRA. http://italk-youtalk.com

If you would like to read more graded readers, please visit our website http://www.italkyoutalk.com

Other Level 1 graded readers include
A Business Trip to New York
A Trip to London
Dear Ellen
Haruna's Story Part 1
Haruna's Story Part 2
Haruna's Story Part 3
Ken's Story Part 1
Ken's Story Part 2
Life is Surprising!
Strange Stories
The Christmas Present
The Old Hospital
We Met Online

ABOUT THE AUTHOR

I Talk You Talk Press is a Japan-based publisher of language textbooks, graded readers and language learning/teaching resources.

Our team is made up of highly experienced language teachers and translators, who have all studied at least one additional language to an advanced level.

This experience enables us to design our materials from the perspective of both the teacher and the learner. We consult with both teachers and language learners when designing our textbooks and graded readers, and test our materials extensively in the classroom before publication.

We are a fast-growing press, and currently publish graded readers for learners of English. We publish new graded readers monthly.

www.ingramcontent.com/pod-product-compliance
Lightning Source LLC
Chambersburg PA
CBHW022348040426
42449CB00006B/769